Because We Are Rivers

Mark Edward Mann

Because We Are Rivers
by
Mark Edward Mann

Published/Designed :   Nicasio Press
Sebastopol, California
www.nicasiopress.com

ISBN: 979-8-9864100-3-6
Printed in the U.S.A.

The imagination is man's power over nature.

Wallace Stevens

Acknowledgements

I would like to acknowledge several people whom, I believe, saved my brother's life and/or loved him like a brother, as well as those who contributed to making this publication of Mark's poetry a reality.

I want to pay tribute to The Ark, and specifically, its Intensive Day Program (IDP), a social services organization in Chicago. Without their love and support of Mark, I am not sure he would have ever pursued his dreams of becoming a writer. Mark's poetry has touched so many lives—from the staff and members of The Ark's IDP, to the many friends who encouraged him throughout the years. A special thank you to Na'ama Wasserman, his psychologist and friend, who supported Mark for more than twenty years. Na'Ama was Mark's rock.

I would also like to affirm the deep relationship between Mark and Rabbi Shlomo Tenenbaum, whose congregation includes members of The Ark. Rabbi Shlomo has known my brother for more than twenty years, and both he and Na'ama became my rock during Mark's illness and subsequent passing. Without them, I would have felt lost, and am truly grateful that Mark was in good hands with his primary cheerleaders. They gave him sage advice and inspired him to follow his passion—poetry. As a way of paying it forward, Mark taught a poetry class at The Ark for the past several years, and inspired all who attended his classes to unleash their own creative juices.

Mark loved to read, and he loved books. Many thanks to Keith Peterson, who owned Selected Works, an iconic bookstore on Chicago's Michigan Avenue, where Mark worked for many years. Mark loved to go to work so he could see both Keith and Hodge, the beloved cat that lived at the bookstore. Mark often collaborated with Keith on his poetry. In 2013 Keith printed Mark's poems in the chapbook *The Essential Distance*.

Just before the pandemic, Mark applied and got accepted to the very prestigious summer program Bread Loaf Writers Conference, in

New England. Even though it had to be held virtually, Mark's talents were recognized and featured at the conference.

One of Mark's close friends, Lisa Pogoff, had a special connection with Mark, and she sent him a poem every day, some of which they discussed at length. Though Lisa and her family live in Minneapolis, Mark visited them occasionally over the years. Thank you, Lisa, for your friendship with Mark. He loved you and spoke to me about you often.

When my brother initially returned to Chicago around 2001, he reconnected with many of his grammar school and high school friends. These friends are all still close today, and Mark spent many weekends out in Skokie hanging out with them. These friends, such as Danny Gitlis, were very supportive of me throughout Mark's illness. I am grateful to have met so many of Mark's friends and swapped stories about my brother.

Special thanks are also due to Rollin Feld, an old friend of Mark, who contacted me after Mark passed away with an offer to publish Mark's poetry. Thank you, Rollin, for your determination in pulling together what you needed to make this book happen. And a singular thanks to Nicasio Press and Laura Duggan, who worked with Rollin to publish this book. I am so appreciative that Mark's works will live on due to the love and respect for him. Thank you all.

Sherrie Mann Foley
August, 2022

Publisher's Note

This book of poetry, published posthumously, has been designed to be faithful as possible to an unpublished PDF file originally prepared by Mark Mann and shared with some of his friends. This book retains his varied choice of capitalization for poem titles and words, rather than standardize them. It also attempts to reconstruct some of the spacing as best as possible, given the source materials. In this way, we hope that the readers can directly experience the heartfelt meaning of the poems and Mark's intent in his original manuscript.

Thanks to the generosity of the sponsors of this book, a portion of the royalties will be donated to The Ark - Intensive Day Program, a non-profit organization in Chicago. For more information about their work, visit their website at https://arkchicago.org/.

Laura Duggan
Publisher, Nicasio Press

Because We Are Rivers

The Road Taken

I veered to the left,
toward Montana,

under an eagle on her way
to Montana and beyond

to the mysterious forest
along the Columbia River.

If I die before I get there,
you can have my bicycle.

Two

My eyes look green,
or my eyes look blue.

I am of two minds,
so for me there are two kinds of you:

one muddying her toes in the garden
for the sake of the sunlit asphodel,

the other sipping tea at the table
in the cool morning light.

I have come a long way only to close my eyes,
but let's not harden our hearts just yet.

Look into my green or look into my blue
and tell me are you in the garden

tending your flowers,
or am I at the table resting with you?

Scooter

every morning
the jewish kid
comes clacking by
on his scooter
headed for
the synagogue to pray
the sidewalk
has a rhythm
every five feet
another line
perfect iambic pentameters
sha-clack
sha-clack
sha-clack
till he gets there
and jumps off
and leaves me
with his poem

A Pretty Nice '7 4 Cutlass

I'm standing here on the curve of the Earth
next to a pretty nice '74 Cutlass.

I don't really like standing here,
so I'm thinking of other things that are curved:

flower petals and hips and hockey pucks, etc.
It's the only thing I know how to do.

If I Were to Paint

If I were to paint
a poem of you

I'd paint the way
you smooth your hair

back over your ears
the way the cords

in your neck
fan down when you turn

the way your lovely hands
rest in your lap

like flowers at rest
in the garden bed

the way you regard
as the mona lisa regards

slightly amused
her leonardo da vinci

A Morning at the Window

the eye through which comes
the light of the moon

vaguely sinking behind
the heap of buildings

now falls on the light of you
and you enter with the river

sliding past the wet trees
under the blue fog

and smoke of my cigarette
on the lip of the ashtray

of another november
here on the earth

and your face lifts
from its sleep and blinks

and asks me what time it is
here in my heart

Guardian Angel

There was a time
when angels ruled the air,
thick as honeybees buzzing in the sun,
but nobody remembers that.

Now, you'd be lucky
if an angel rang your bell
to ask for a cool drink of water—
the way was long and arduous,

a turbulent flight, he says,
and he'd appreciate it if he could
take a hot bath and maybe a small meal.
He comes empty-handed,

no message to change your life,
nothing, and all you can think
is how white he remains in his poverty,
how tiny the trembling wings.

one baltimore

two baltimores
three baltimores four
when in the course
of human events
it becomes necessary
my fellow baltimores
lend me your ears
I pledge allegiance
to the flag of the
united states of baltimore
whose ugliness is
commensurate with
the beauty of the chesapeake
for one people to dissolve
the political bands
which have connected them to another
and to the republic
for which it stands
truth justice
and the baltimore way
keep baltimore beautiful
where the streets are paved with gold
as baltimorean as apple pie
one baltimore under god
and its confusion of rage
indivisible
burning burning
with liberty and justice
we hold these truths baltimore baltimore
to be self-evident
for all god
shed his grace on thee

Kettle, River, Bird

The kettle steams but does not whistle.
The steam vanishes like soul
into the afterlife.

Over the edge of the river,
the alder trees lean and bristle
with red-winged blackbirds.

A falcon in the fog hunting along the river
is true insofar as it is
permanently opposed to the lie.

Steam rises from the kettle.
The peace eluding me moves with the river.
The blackbirds panic and leave the trees.

In the heart of night, the only thing left
is the river moving through the city
like a rabbi through his dark synagogue.

The Language of Flowers

This little I know
of the language of flowers:

a subject of lily,
a predicate of rose,

syllables in the heart
of the same desire

that burned the phoenix
before the phoenix rose.

O water the lily
and water the rose

with that leaping
all-too-human fire!

The Total Eclipse

the moon came between the sun
and the cement truck

rotating on its axis

just like the
ancients predicted

That Was Close

you never know when
a little wind is going to

blow you right off
the roof of the

prudential building

Lions and Trampolines

I wasn't impressed
with the little bit of rain
that fell last night

so instead of
an erotic poem about you
I wrote this

it's about lions
bouncing on trampolines
as you can see

Dvořák

when the world was full of gods
we had no need of Dvořák

were quite content with Pythagorean
harmonies and tinkling tunes

the music of the spheres
and so forth

but jesus h christ
every time you turned around

you were tripping over one god
or another

they were in our heads
up to their elbows

like movie stars
and every night of your life

spent at the Sunset Drive-In
that's where Dvořák comes in

Memorial Park

They've held it for me since fifty-three
when my grandmother bought it
for two-hundred-and-eight dollars.

They knew I'd be coming someday.
On the way in I noticed a pair
of swans drifting on the pond

along a road that wound through a gauntlet
of shade trees, home to a few songbirds,
some pastoral planner's idea of the idyllic.

It's still there, of course,
one slot north of my grandfather
in a row crowded with low stones,

names and dates, nothing else,
his no more memorable than the others
but for the fact that I share it,

and he dead the year I was born
like a runner in the 4 X 4
handing off the baton for the final leg.

I can't get over the swans.

I Came to the Grave of Mary Lee

I came to the grave of Mary Lee
at the end of the river
where the heart slowly empties into the sea,

and there I watched the water move
and merge with wider form
as though finally to prove

that all equations are magic tricks
and all our certainties sopping wet
she's lain there alone since sixty-six.

I came away from the yard and passed
no wiser, not deviating from the norm,
but drowning in the hollows of the sea at last

was moved by how the dead lay
so near the river,
wondered what I should say

if someone asked what I had found.
In ground where the river slips into the sea,
I found the stone of Mary Lee.

A Poem For The Five-Year Old Daughter I Never Had

I give you all the roses in my heart,
that roseberry tree.

Here they are.

Add them to the roses already in you
one by one,
or two by two,
it doesn't much matter,

until you become a place of roses
and the rows of roses
become a garden of you.

And soon they'll add up
to a roseberry tree.

And later, when it's time
and you mean it,
(and time always comes
to the roseberry tree)

you'll give away roses
two by two or three by three

it doesn't much matter
wheeeeeeeeee!

Occasionally A Falcon/ or A Winter Funeral

the tentacles of the frozen trees
bear the bowls of nests aloft

and occasionally a falcon
or a red-tailed hawk

balances on a branch
in the shocking wind

so there is life
on the move among the dead

and this in our sorrow is thy sign
I note today in passing

for tomorrow I may be colder
my senses stunned

and grasping at absurdity
be blind to the scene

be deaf to the falcon's
eternal cry

The Day Room

She fills her afternoons
near the aquarium,
watches the fish flick by
this way and that over a few shells

at rest in the blue gravel.
Not much room in that sea
to wander, not much room
on that side of the glass.

The nurse checks in on her
every now and then
in case she slips off or
disappears in a dream—

not much room to wander we have,
old women on the cusp:
the sea if we choose,
or the stars if we must.

Go

go where you will not go
find the flowers

in the nothing there
return with one in your hand

give it light give it water
give it a name

what a handsome flower
people will say

how lucky you are
to have it

but tell them
where you got it

tell them you went
where no one will go

and you will change
the way they think

Spring Comes Pale

Spring
comes pale
and stupefied

to the lawns
and bushes
and empty trees

like an idiot
institutionalized
for life, released

A Morning Walk

This morning I paused
over the north branch
to watch two brown ducks
gliding on the river,

disappearing below me
beneath the arch of the bridge
like teenagers into
the tunnel of love,

emerging with the current
on the other side.
Sure I'm unhappy,
but there are still things to see.

Detached, a shadow
moves down the length of the river.
It once belonged to a red-tailed hawk.

After Life

Soul is a light and airy thing
like steam that vanishes above a pot,
but grieve that you had and now have not
a summer, a fall, a winter and spring.

Upon Learning Of The Holocaust

Before I put my fingers in the fire
the stove stood
as a place of hard wonder,
the keeper of the flame.

Later, I learned there is a fire
that can incinerate soul,
a fire invisible for invisible soul.

Beyond stove to soul
this nauseating smoke,
 and perhaps a woman
walking her pomeranian.

Anagnorisis

I do not know the name
of this flower in my hand—
white petals, yellow heart.

Death always has a name,
I suppose, and cannot be held
like a kitten in one's hand.

Where the river disappears
into the sea, that is death,
the end of ambiguity,

and it is mighty, and a becoming.
Didn't I think of heaven just yesterday,
how the water ascends invisibly?'

Yee chis nameless flower in my hand
itself names something.
Touch it and you'll feel it, the shock.

Hamburger Telegram

tonight I'm eating
a delicious hamburger

and thinking how
for seven days last week

I thought how pretty you are
in the summer

it was like seven fireflies winking
in the dark august heat

Noah's Ark

I left you what I think
is a poem
stuck to the door

of the refrigerator
with a vivid blue magnet
depicting noah's ark.

the poem like the magnet
is at a farther remove from reality
than you're accustomed to.

it might not correspond
to anything at all.

you'll see it before you
retrieve the butter

or the milk
or the oranges.

Late Night Fireplace

Having no science,
I occasionally wonder

why it's so dark
among the fires

of so many stars,
even the Earth at rest

in it's empty bowl,
like a cueball scratched

in the corner pocket,
is surrounded.

Prayers to the Name
forbidden to the tongue,

to the innumerable holes
His vast vectors pierce.

Let's finish these chocolates
while we're still young.

New Mexico

I was driving a road
through the heart of New Mexico,
when up ahead I saw a pool of water
shimmering in the heat.

It's an oasis, I thought,
because my great thirst
had driven me mad.

Sure enough, it was
ten thousand tarantulas
flooding the road.

I drove back to Gallup
to get a Dr. Pepper.
It's always a goddamn mirage.

Dry Roses

Seven homeless guys
are hanging upside down
over the sidewalk

in front of my building.
It's like a dazzling circus finale,
the Flying So-and-So's.

They're working without a net.

My girlfriend is drying
the seven red roses I gave her
for Valentine's Day upside

down from the chandelier.
I know what you're thinking,
but she's not crazy.

She doesn't want to die.

A Cloudy Day In October

The wave that from
the black bottom rises
can kill a man

as it kisses the mouth
of the empty beach.
Two swimmers arrive

and plunge like porpoises
into this sea.
They swim out, arching

through the waves
that from the bottom gather
and slide on the yellow sand.

They keep going,
unreasonably,
beyond the breakers.

The same water in which they swam
that evening fell
all over the city.

Sonnet 3

A woman's art knows what to do with death,
giving birth to that which is born to die,
loveliest she is where dead roses lie
when God holds his breeze like a man holds his breath.
And she herself born in that calamity
knows something of part and something of whole—
What is body without a woman's soul?
A moment apart from eternity?
Muscular Michelangelo had this,
could free a flower from the marble of
March, turn winter's root to the rose's love,
and cool to the touch is April's first kiss.
A woman's art knows what to do with death,
when God holds his breeze like a man holds his breath.

Hanukkah Divertimento

i once held out
for a solid week
squeezing toothpaste
from a completely empty

tube of aquafresh
so it's possible
that's all i'm saying
even god was against me

Dry Roses

women know what to do
with death when they see it

I would not have her
without that wonder

among all the stately shadows
her eye on the mystery

like spring
that muscular michelangelo

who frees the flower
from the marble of march

and cool to the touch
was april's first kiss

and when the summer had ended
she harvested roses

and hung them
upside down from the chandelier

like windchimes
until they were as thirsty as paper

like spring that rainy rapunzel
letting down her golden hair

which looked that fall
like the last forsythia

still yellow in the yard
behind the presbyterian church

and sometimes, she says,
we make do without death

if god holds his breeze
like a man holds his breath

Science Fiction Movie

This light left the sun
eight minutes ago.

It just got here.

I'm walking in it on my way
to the matinee.

When I go inside,
it's lights out.

When I come back,
it's still there.

We live
in an interesting place.

The Evening News

the tattoo down the back
of the woman's arm
was the scottish proverb
'waves will rise on silent water'

the disabled woman's arm
hovered hypnotically
after she dropped her coins
into the farebox

a cardinal sat
in the birch tree
a drop of blood
on a woman's white arm

when i woke up this morning
my left arm was asleep
like a woman
under me

after months of searching
i finally found my
birth certificate

One Can Always Imagine A Fire

Like a blind Polish girl
out walking her pomeranian,
one must imagine if one is to see.

Before I put my fingers in the fire
the stove stood as a place of hard wonder,
 \the nothing from which fire came.

Later, I learned there is a fire
that can incinerate soul,
a fire invisible for invisible soul.

And beyond on the continent
there burned a fire
of sizzling congregation.

The flame of sunlight across her cheek.
The flare of her image in the glittering glass.
The spark that ignites the streetdancer's feet.

Belmont Harbor

The summer is ending,
and the boats tug
toward ice

where God is dead,
History dead,
and Nature, too.

To sing is to speak
but to speak is not to sing,
so shall I sing elaborately

or speak in single syllables
to comprehend this unmooring?
What is left for the pen to do?

The Last Time I Saw David

He was gone just seconds
before I got there
and I sank into the hospital chair
at the end of his bed
and I reached and held his foot in my hand,

and before he stopped breathing
his heart was beating so hard
the whole bed shook,
was what my cousin said,

and all I could think
was how smooth and small
his foot was there in my hand
and I thought it was like
holding a hummingbird,
and I let it go.

I'd never seen a soul
become a hummingbird before,
darting from flower
to flower to flower.

A Man Reading On The Bus

Blind, the man
near the front of the bus
gazes at the beautiful woman
across from him.

Or, he does not gaze.
In any case, she's
used to being beheld.

The book like any book
lies flat in his lap.
His hand moves quickly
over the white pages

like a dragonfly.
The words are the delight
of his fingertips.

Tisha B'Av

Five thousand years of fire and fear
have brought us to this
garden-green patch of Illinois
overlooking the Fox River.

On the far bank,
red-winged blackbirds
crowd the branches
of alder trees,

and the boat we came by
bobs on the river,
empty for us
to return upstream.

Say aleph in silence,
most ancient of vowels,
speak water to fire,
my love, my love.

Because you are like
a flower in my hand,
I pick you clematis
on this the saddest day of the year.

Icarus

the sun seduced ambitious icarus
like a 60 watt lightbulb
seduces a moth

don't kid yourself
it was a trick
his wax wings melted
half way home
the feathers would not hold
and he dropped
flipping and flapping
into the sea
the tide eventually
washing his bloated body
up on the beach
with rhe other shells
and of all the crazy things
a pine cone
my schnauzer
didn't know
what to make of it
it was horrible
he lay there
like a tarot card
the drowned youth

and how would it be
if Madame so-and-so
her blackfire eyes
 burning for your fate
laid that on the table?

The Magnolia Tree

my mother loved
her magnolia tree

first it burst
into fanatical bloom

soon thereafter
its petals fell

the grass was white
and the garden bed

she watered the pots
on the window sill

she said
the petals have fallen

and touched her hair
above her ear

because nature
like grandma and god

was dead

Love Song In June

Not a peep

from the puny parakeet
in the cage of my heart

so I opened the gate
but he would not leave.

Secretly you sang there
such lovely songs

perched by the side
of the pale parakeet

who gave no song
but you sang there alone

as though you sang for me
on your own leafy bough

in the cage of my heart.
I've never told anyone

how your singing sings
my eyes open each day

or how you sing and soar
in my stony sleep

or of the moody and
puzzling parakeet

who keeps to himself
in the cage of my heart.

I can't go on like this.

The Inner Life

In the poem I'm reading
much is made of the vivid old smell
of dead leaves burning.

The speaker is walking home in October
and remembers the leaves in her neighborhood
crackling blackening smoking.

Then without warning I'm in the poem
and it's late in the spring but my nose
is fogged with the smoke of the leaves

and I'm reading license plates
as I make my way home down Kedzie Avenue
along the north branch of the Chicago River.

I like the way she pinned me there
like a prize specimen framed under glass.
I love the way she left me no choice.

Every Morning

the birds
in my neighborhood

make their music
at three

they dawn dark
with dawn-dark song

crying out
from the branches

beyond the leaves
and it's always the same

confusion of song
when your woman

finally leaves you
and it's everywhere

on the radio
breaking your heart

An Evening in February

It is hard to hear
the winter wind
rushing along the

snowgray street
and around the frozen trees
and not believe in something.

The wind moves metaphysically
like a ghost in the house
lifting curtains and
leaving doors ajar.

It is winter.
The wind blows invisibly.
The poplars are impregnable,
as hard as they will ever be.

The Mountain

The mountain here
at the end of my life
is a stoneheap of things
I wanted to say to you.

They're all part of the mountain now,
words like deeply and vividly
in the rock of my heart, words like
I love you like no other, stone.

The monolith stands there, a giant
of truths that eluded me—
that's the way it has to be
for there to be a mountain at all—

but it's not the kind of mountain
one climbs or admires,
it pierces no clouds,
no white skirt upon its peak.

In the valley of the brute
all you can do
is tremble and blink.

The Poetry

Is it thought and feeling
and faith itself

or is it a random speck
a grain of sand

an irritation
in the mind

that later becomes
a poem on a page?

One must have a thought of the pearl,
and believe it.

One must have rm emotion of iridescence,
and think it.

One must have a faith of the sea,
and feel it.

Two Horses

The eyes in their tireless desire
finally rest on a chestnut mare
calmly grazing a field

not far from the road
north of Los Angeles.
Her colt nearby practices his paces,

moving with gravitas about and about her.
The colt has nothing to do with the darkness of the sea,
and I am young with him today, blind to

the sea beyond the hills at the end of the world,
it's heavenly heavings not of his flesh,

not of himself and not of his kind,
though in the evening,
when the beach empties,

people will walk their horses
along the edge of the sea, which is the edge of the sky.

The sea withdraws again and again,
leaving its deadly line in the sand.
The colt flicks his head in the bright air.
The broad muscle of the mare's neck extends to the field.

Shikaakwa

in the chicago of the mind
I peel away the stockyards
the bloodstink the manure the hide
fogging the nostrils

I shut the mouths of rusting boxcars
littering the southside freightyards

I uproot front yards back yards bungalows
I yank up the streets and avenues
beat them like rugs the dust descending

I tornado the buildings
they tumble and crash
I sweep them away

I crack all the bridges
they thunder into themselves

I blur the distinctions

I snip the girders that keep
the el tracks aloft

I hurricane the harbors
and all the pretty boats disappear

I crumple all the fences
and all the eagles return

I erase all the signs

I delete all references to the big-shouldered city
that toddling town

I send all the people packing
I leave no stone unturned

I leave the flowers
the trees
the beaches
the wind

and when I am once again a sauk brave
knowing nothing of heraclitus
I step into the same river twice

and extend my arm like a ladle
to drink of the river

and lift to my lips
 a handful of water

so cold so cold

I Give You All The Roses

I give you all the roses in my heart.

Here they are.

Add them to the roses
already in you
one by one
or two by two,
it doesn't much matter,

until you become
a place of roses
and the rows of roses
become a garden of you.

Don't think you have to reciprocate
any time soon.
They're your roses now,
all yours,

but give one to me
when I am dying;
one will do.

An Address To The Lord On New Year's Day

I woke in the darkness
just before dawn
to tell you what I feel.

The darkness is like
a quiet synagogue
around me
a holy place.

No fancy words
or mendacious magnitudes
or clever ironies
will suffice.

I miss you
because I
love you.

Your dawnlight
seeps in
around the edge
of the windows.

I wish you could see it.

An Assignment For The Thursday Poetry Class

to make that perfect
yearned-for sense
that pitch-perfect poem

using all the right words
that body of lines
that lives in itself

outside the mind
with no need of mind
and its profundum

the gaze of an animal
somewhere in a camouflage
of yellow grass

a movement in the bushes
a dead leaf crackling
under its stealth

prized in the west
for its dazzling hide

The Flowers Of Heaven

Here lies the name
forbidden to the tongue.

What is it we lose
when we lose such a god?

At the farthest transport
of the imagination,

beyond the white visions
and breezy golden fields,

I found strange flowers
to pick for you.

They will complete you
for the time being,

like a decoration of clouds
here and there in an empty sky,

and then the image in the mind
long after they wither.

I don't know what they're called,
there was no one there to name them,
but here they are.

'If l were equal to the things I know'

If l were equal to the things I know,
things chiseled from the marble block,

I'd see my body, that broken stone,
smooth and trembling in its jello mold.

The Earth is small and trembling, too,
but she is like the god in her

lonely turn through the emptiness,
the horrible emptiness

His vast vectors pierce,
and I am much smaller, infinitely so.

Rain As an Idea

The rain comes down in Euclidean cords
on the alder trees along the river.

One may say something of the findern flowers
there beneath the umbrella of trees,

or not speak at all. One need not speak.
One need not even find the flowers

beautiful and of a surpassing order
on the ground there in the fundamental rain,

six white petals with round yellow hearts.
The rain will go where the river goes.

On an alder branch in the rain-rinsed air
a wet speckled blackbird bristles and thinks

the way a river thinks on its way to the sea.
The rain in you is the river in me.

Like Paul Klee's line and restless dot

Like Paul Klee's line and restless dot
a life is a moment
that went for a walk.

At the moment, though,
all is still, unwavering,

and I notice the
grain of the mahogany
of my Mozart-playing
music box; the stain

on my desk that looks
just like Lorenzo de Medici;

the streaks of sunlight
crossing my blinds.

There's more, and more,
and infinitely more,
but surely that's sufficient.

RED-FEATHERED BIRD

Something separates the note from the noise,
Image from the veil of things;

Song is the swerve of syllable,
Singer a vessel with wings.

AFTER DIAGNOSIS

- for Nancy Marie Wilson

When the snow comes early
And you are touched by winter
And the only thing left stirring is

A bay mare moving like a
River through the white field,
You know then that you, too,

Are a river running quietly
Out to the sea. The snow descends.
The mare breathes and steams

And balks in the frost,
Her river-dark tail flicking at flakes,
A river behind her, a river to come.

TO BE IS TO BE PERCEIVED

A glitter of sunlight through the leaves
is a fact of leaves flickering in the broad

sunlight, an act of believing what can be seen.
Under the sparkle of sunlight piercing the leaves

the blue cat sits and licks its paw.
This is true in all possible worlds.

We don't only see, then,
the things we only want to see.

The sunlight falls like snow through the leaves.
The blue cat moves on, turning for one last

look at you under the leaves, under
the falling flakes gone glittering down.

AFTERNOON IN THE PARK
for Edna

A blue balloon dancing along
at the end of a string tied to a child's wrist,
or a blue poem tied to a river,

to a stallion, to a red-tailed hawk
Sooner or later she must lose it
like the last note to leave the violin,

its moment come round to resolve
the crescendo, suspended
in the air of the ear, the final stroke,

and the blue balloon, the blue poem,
also will rise to the end of the line,
to the white monotony of heaven

where nothing more is possible,
where we no longer speak
the language we leave behind.

Two Poems

tonight
i stayed up late

and wrote you
a love poem

this isn't it
this is a poem

i wrote a
little later

about how thin
and twiggy

the ash trees look
by thanksgiving

TO GOD, OR SOMEONE LIKE THAT

"Now the General was consulting God, or someone like that."
- Robert Graves

Who whirls the wind, who reds the rose,
who fits the moon to a fingernail,
but you, O sky to my soul.

Unless I've made an egregious mistake.
Having a soul, that is, an inner air.
Perhaps it's not there, not there at all,

for me to consecrate to high purpose.
And maybe you, the arch totalitarian,
are at heart agnostic too, not able

to know yourself necessarily,
nor fear yourself in proper obeisance.
I think I grasp the paradox of you:

you're like the perhaps sentence,
This is not a sentence-
true if it's false, and false if it's true.

Don't you ring both true and false, false and true?
One must have a sense of humor about
these things to offset all the horrors

you've set before our incredulous eyes.
Fodder for historians, I suppose,
but never mistaken for the rose.

THE FALLS

Waters rush and tumble forth
until the quiet of winter

works its way into the heart.
At some moment the falls

freeze solid into a trunk
of ragged ice, the falling

caught in the falling,
all falling down.

Everything falls to the cold—
I remember helping

my grandmother
into the sleeves of her sweaters—

but I find a peace here
on the white land by the falls,

in the red beat of the heart
among the frozen trees.

RAIN FICTION

The pock pock pock
Of the rain dropping

On the window sill is
Something I usually listen to

Instead of writing
poetry

But tonight I'm not listening
To the rain

I'm listening
To you in the kitchen

Shaving apples
In your slippers and

The silence you make
Is of the rain-rinsed air

LOVE

a sea-slant of sunlight
above and beneath

surface and fathom
a cage and its heart

the red dancer dancing
in the cage of its art

MY FATHER, THE FIRST DEAD GOD

My father, the first dead god,
lay naked and neglected
at the foot of his throne,

he who had moved
like a great shadow across the lawn,
his breeze held like breath.

My father sank to his death
through the thick salt sea, befitting a mariner

who remembered what so many forget,
what to keep holy in a shattered world.

My father bled out on the battlefield,
well beyond saving, a goner.

A heart attack flattened him one April day,
when spring frees the flower
from the marble of March,

like a page of concerto torn from its score
a piece of it there, then emptiness, the
flamboyant crescendo, the palpable rest.

FORSYTHIA

The forsythia exclude me.
All I can do

is shed light on the yellow,
show it to others,

let others see it
in the light incomplete,

partial, movable.
The chaos of yellow flowers

that comprises the whole
might be the stars

ancient peoples
mythologically fixed.

It's a lifetime of work.
It is never enough.

NO SMALL THING

A speckled blackbird
with the sun on its back
hopping on the lawn,
is my neighbor's
freckled daughter
playing hopscotch
on the sidewalk,
is Aldrin leaping
in the dust of the moon.

It's no small thing
to sit here dreaming,
observing the bird,
the hopping girl,
the playful astronaut,
and not be able to say
with certainty that one
does not inhabit the other.

Yet I cannot say they are all
discrete entities either,
à la the ardent philosopher,
parsed out in spades with
great space between them.

It's a bleeding of
one thing into another,
one red two and two red three,
the heart's salt sea
slipping over the sand.

SNOWFALL

The field receives the snow
like a woman powdering her face.

A moment before the woman didn't exist
and a moment after she didn't matter

because the snow dominates the air today,
a fullness of white, the falling snow.

One may have second thoughts,
one may have another knowledge

beside the being of the self.
It is winter and the field fills

anciently, anciently beyond the self.
She doesn't tell you everything.

PINES IN GEORGIA

The pine is to Georgia
what the line is to Euclid—

the stiff geometry, the piercing pine,
bristling in such forests

that green the red land,
realer than the realest paraphrase.

It is raining. Under thunder,
the pine trees stand. Unlike Georgia,

Euclid has no lightning
to cleave the dark line.

TRADING EPISTEMOLOGIES

She said there was something behind the stars,
a fuller light that falls on all things.
She doesn't really know that,

but I believed her anyway.
I lied and told her the Sauk believed
that because we are rivers, when we

step into the river
we are stepping into ourselves,
and then we see what rivers see:

the branches of the alder trees
along the banks bristling
with red-winged blackbirds;

The sunlight breaking across the water
the lean boats tugging at the crumbling pine.
And because we are rivers we carry the sky,

and it flows and runs with us downstream,
rippling down to the end of the line
where the heart slowly empties into the sea.

And because we are rivers everything repeats
in resemblance, beyond the reach of reason,
and thus beyond our surfaces, our depths,

our waters, ourselves,
the falcon circling is beheld.

THE WIND THAT IS COMING

When the wind finds its way through winter's glaze
lines will shift accordingly,
boundaries will adjust and readjust,
and those undone will rise newly wrought.

Even the wind of a world so reduced
is our wind,
yet the savagery that drove
the leaves to their ruin

a few dead months ago
is the same that comes to green the season
along the boughs,
just as fierce is that desire.

A sapling bends in the evening wind—
already it's like an old woman
preparing for sleep,
her destruction complete.

CORNFLOWERS

I set out to write you a love poem,
but instead I wrote this.

It's to you, but it's not about you.
It's about the cornflowers

I saw in a field yesterday,
so bright and dancing blue.

The little I know of cornflowers
is the little I know of you.

I didn't have to write this poem,
but now that it exists,

you may find it among my possessions
and think, what a strange flower

to find here among the books
on the floor, among the laundry and all the rest.

What a strange flower, I wrote,
what a strange blue flower of you.

WATERFALL

Make no mistake,
no matter how certain you are,
you will suffer

in the enclosing darkness,
in the leaving of the light, if only by virtue of

human memory,
of the sense of all
you will leave behind.

This is the loss you'll understand,
measured out in favorite people,
the kiss of blue sky above you,

on square green lawns
in the summer of your days.

Nothing more will matter,
but what you lose.

And with this suffering,
you will come to comprehend—

poised on the rock of the holy
the fierce and furious

emptying of the end.

AT FAITH'S FUNERAL

They take everything
with them, the dead:
philosophy, recipes, algebra.
You learn nothing from them,

unless they're accompanied
by a red-tailed hawk
muscling through the air,
its great wings propelling it on.

(A red-tailed hawk
appeared in the sky
and crossed over our
little gathering

and away to the crust
of apartment buildings
beyond the edge
of the cemetery).

Call it her soul
finally taking its flight.
You'll remember that
for the rest of your life.

EPITAPH

Learn not from these bones
of Mark Edward Mann,
whose flesh once could
but no longer can.
Look elsewhere, and live!

A NORTHERN EXPOSURE

here in the north
it's spring again and

not winter and
the leaves have risen

and all and vast the
wet green shoots and

every flesh comes freshly sprung
of frozen time, of sovereign sleep.

WHAT YOU HELD

In the picture of you
holding your shih-tzu

you look lovely
but a little sad

peeking out of
the white glare

of the light leaking
into your living-room

some old sorrow perhaps
that you don't talk about

and that too you held tight
like your happy little dog

that too

THE ABOMINABLE SNOWMAN

There is an utterance
asleep on my tongue
that eludes me like the

abominable snowman,
lonely and haunting
the cold hard hills.

It might be of a flower there,
or a river, or the
touch of your gentle hand,

or all these things gathered
into one true word,
or something else entirely,

yet all faith makes us
wait and wait:
I think what sleeps might just be

the sheen the sun leaves
on the back of a blackbird,
or a word the color of a cloud full of rain.

Night Rain

I lose myself in you
the way rain
loses itself in a river,

the way a river
loses itself in the sea.

So that all may see,
let lightning burst
and crack upon us
its crackling beam.

I like that, you said,
the rain in you
is the river in me.

SNOW IN THE CITY

A stalwart chestnut
tugs a carriage of tourists
through the white streets, the
slow tramp of shod hooves.

Cars whisper along,
but yield to the mare
and the secret river
mapped inside her.

In March she'll lumber
through the runoff,
pulling wet newlyweds
or families from Ohio,

yet in the book of heaven
the snow descends,
keeps on falling page after page.

So there are words for it,
for this moment of world,
which stand there for the taking.

And yet, there is mystery.
Tell me of that map unique,
and tell me of the river.

THERE MUST BE SOMETHING PERFECT

There must be something perfect
pressed between us
when we hold each other
on this bed, something
thin like a leaf in a book.

Tonight is a wild bird
your small hand releases,
which will never return.

This time, when we separate to sleep,
we fall open like pages,
and there it is, the leaf.

Farewell To Paradise

With the end
of the world
so near,
two beautiful bays
in the late afternoon
moving like rivers
through the
white field
back to the barn
by the black road
that runs to Oconomowoc,
Wisconsin, is a
staggering
loss.

For Avery, On Her Leaving

Because we are rivers, we see
what rivers see—

the branches of the alder trees
along the banks bristling

with red-winged blackbirds,
the sunlight breaking across the water,

the white boats
tugging at old pine docks.

Because we are rivers,
we go on like this forever,

turning only to wave our goodbyes.
Rivers are famous for waving goodbye.

An Ostrich

Like all ghosts
our ghost was impregnable.

We didn't really understand him,
so we took him to the circus.

He approved of the bareback riders
and the flying trapeze,

but he couldn't clap
because he had no hands.

He was like an ostrich
trying to break into a Cadillac.

The Thing In Itself

she's covered inside
with chrysanthemums

so it's easy
to understand

why she sings
around leaves

like the black mask
silver bullets

and white stallion
inside Clayton Moore

what else could he do?
who else could he be?

DESIDERATUM

My heart is hung with talismans
like icicles from the eaves,
and I think of you all winter long.

I wonder if my parents in heaven
are still divorced, or are they, as
Emerson said, by one music enchanted?

After summer the leaves get crisp.
And far away, far from me,
the sea and its darker angels heave.

Make No Little Plans

Nature observed is never pristine
(the human eye changes everything),
but if the city were suddenly gone

maybe the eagles would return,
and maybe the herons, too,
to live upon the ruin.

And every day I would wake
to the revelation of an eagle
 muscling her way into the sky

with meat in her talons,
or dive-bombing fish in the old river.
And in that waking is my end.

The imagination, then, always finds paint
for the things it replaces,

as do the herons upon their sticks,
asleep in the marsh among the leg-like reeds.

Valentine's Day Sonnet

when the dreamer
in my chest

dreams about love
it dreams about women

when it dreams about women
it dreams about you

it doesn't beat harder
like you'd think it would

it doesn't know any sentences
or phrases or fancy words

every night it's a whisper
that wakes me

like the sea in a shell
this syllable of you

A LOVE POEM

I seldom argue
with the proposition

that darkness will always
return to the heart

yet even when
I got seasick

over the gunwale
of the little boat

on the twilit lake
near the Fox River

and threw up
three banana daiquiris

that looked like an omelet
floating in brown butter

I was thinking of you

After Traveling by Night

I saw all the stars there are to see
 one night while pissing
on the side of the road
into a field of Nebraska wheat.

Nearly human in the things they sang,
the inhuman stars were like
a choir without a chorister.

One strains to remember
but it eludes the ear,
this murmuring in the heart,
this music of the spheres.

THINGS

Williams stands
in the white gravel

by the
garbage cans

in the alley behind
the empty

episcopalian
church.

DRIVING HOME THROUGH ILLINOIS

Out of nothing something comes:
a weather of wheat bowing as one wheat
under wine-dark wind. It is September.

The sun rises on the wind rushing over
the roots of the trees. If she speaks,
I cannot say it is not the cry

of a bird who lives in the wind,
who in the wind sings anciently,
anciently, beyond the lyre.

Somewhere between the tractor and barn
she stretches to catch the last of the stars
like a deer to leaves about to fall.

DAYS OF AWE

The spaniel on the porch lifts her black nose
to behold a sound only she can distinguish—

the sound of a few maple leaves,
perhaps, trembling in the trees,

or a distant car coming to a stop,
or bats in flight against the atmosphere.

It would kill us to hear so much,
to hear everything out there,

yet we go on listening as if,
across the summer and on through the fall,

and further still,
we hear dearly a crying out

against that far and final convergence,
the vanishing point, the risen road.

Claim it as the cry of one's very birth,
Magnificent Man, suddenly recalled.

Settling back into the distance of sleep,
the dog hears nothing it cannot know.

The Magnolia Tree

My mother loves her magnolia tree
which stands in the yard
at the back of the house.

Each year it bursts into astonishing bloom
over and above the uncertainty
of an uncertain time.

Then all its white petals fall.

That last year
she was watering the pots on the window sill,
and she said, the petals are falling,

and she touched the hair above her ear,
not quite knowing
what to make of her misery.

Valentine

after all the rain in my heart
one young rose
for you

IGNIS FATUUS

The lights deceive, are meant to deceive,
yet we persist in the experience,
striving toward some illumination of
form in the airglow, some outline in the
shifting light we can identify,
but the lights continue to reconceive
themselves, reflecting, dispersing, the
ongoing aurae behaving as shadows,
away from the permanent, a vanishing.

Plato had his cave, and perhaps he was right—
what shadow cannot be mistaken for light,
and light conversely mistaken for shade?
Yet light was very much simpler then.
Light such as Agamemnon sent kindling
into the night across the chain of hills,
signaling finally the fall of Troy.
And what old watchman, drunk at his post,
would not hurry the news to his bitter queen?

OF A PICTURE OF MY FATHER

Of a picture of my father,
my first dead god,
my mother said: He looks gray,

and a heart attack drowned him
the following May,
according to her prophecy.

Now soul is a light and buoyant thing,
equal to the air in the lungs
according to the book,

and so we vanish quietly
to crickets still whistling
their watery song,

but the book holds the bones
of no drowned youth.
A god's soul rips and rages away.

DESIDERATUM

My heart is hung with talismans
like icicles from the eaves,
and I think of you all winter long.

Somewhere there is a summer sea
fit for feeling and enlarging upon,
rather than this ice in the leaden light

of a late January afternoon. And though
I am ground to the sky and sky to the sea,
in the middle of nowhere one will dream.

Yet I affirm that contrafact—
that after summer the light descends
to return December's frozen beam.

Let all dreams end where all dreams start,
where the sea and its colder angels part.

LOVE POEM WITH WEATHER

Talk about weather
when you talk about love.

Let the light come green,
smell rain in the air,

because I've noticed this about you:
When we talk about weather

and we really mean love,
your eyes fill with rain.

Your lovely green eyes
fill with lovely green rain

like skies filled with water
that never does fall.

But it's winter now,
and tomorrow the snow.

Then speak of the angels
who will melt in your hair.

YOU WOULD HAVE ROSES

You would have roses
rather than poems
celebrating your beauty

or laying claim to your love,
but I can't help
writing things down

because poems perfect
the real,
each iteration an

unwithering magnitude
let loose in the world,
and all forever changed.

See how flawlessly these roses unfold,
the beads of red water,
the fragrant red air?

In Memoriam Mary Lee

I used to help
my grandmother into the
 sleeves of her sweaters

when it was cold
in the room

at the end of the river
where the heart
slowly empties into the sea.

Ars Poetica At 3 am

It was too late for Mozart,
and I in the silence

could only guess
what songs slept

in the hearts of the birds
outside in the trees.

That's how it is
this far from light.

September Serenade

you have some
nice things in your head:

the mahatma snoozing
in the barcalounger,

for example,

and the kid fiddling
with the yahtzee dice.

you have nice hair,
too, very nice.

a little leaf
is caught in your curls.

nothing is ever lost on you.

The Red Poppy

Each year I wait
for five days of this:

blood of the flower,
fire of the heart.

In sleep I remember
it is you I will miss.

This Page Left Blank

this page left blank
intentionally

no scratchy poem
no spicy paragraph
no paraphrase for posterity

a great white rehearsal it is
to have nothing more to say

no high cone of light
to illuminate the afterlife

but the sum of all colors
this white wilderness
this immensity

I stare into it
lost
like a girl in a mirror
searching her face

she's beautiful

October Redux

In the Fall
everything begins
to disappear.

I can't find
a single flower
to pick for you.

I'm getting older
and there is grief
in my heart.

Sunday Dawn

from last evening's
fiery fall

comes cool light rising
over the distant woods

and rather
than nothing

there is something
again

and the resemblances
rise again

from deeper light
of like or as

and something
as real as sunday

settles on the
city

like a hawk on her
nest

Homage To W.C.W.

I am not
wise but I
understand
completely

the beads
of rainwater
on the skin
of the rose

that leans away
from the
chainlink
fence.

Dear Sweet Francine

After having been lost for days
in the denuding heat
of the Sonoran desert,

I in my rawness
suddenly became
a holy Chiricahua warrior

named Ice Cream Truck,
who haunted the land,
and drank of the saguaro.

Chicago is just a memory now,
my beloved Eliza waiting on the porch,
and waiting my spaniel, dear sweet Francine.

FIREFLIES

The yard where the sisters played today
stands empty in the evening.
One can tell they've been here
by the mudpie they left behind
to dry on the card table, but now
they've gone home to the third floor
and are missing the fireflies.
The fireflies revolve so slowly around me,
winking first here, then there, then there.

As a child, I sought to arrest that movement,
snatching them out of the night air
and clapping them into mason jars.
Now, many summers into my life,
I let them go.
I like to think they wink for a woman
I secretly loved, but that's a mere conceit.
I'm utterly alone and ignorant.
I don't know how fireflies bear light in their bones.

The Things You Lose

Anything that can fit in a pocket:
keys, coins, your lighter, that
tiny bottle of nitroglycerin,
phone numbers, bus passes,
wallets, the names of acquaintances
who knew you young.

When you lose your job
and you get evicted, you're
liable to lose some history:
the 48-star American flag that
graced your grandfather's casket, t
he postcards from the French girl
who loved him during World War I,
the picture of your grandmother
and her twelve-year-old twin,
the passport that brought her here
in twenty-three.

And then the metaphysics:
your way there, your way back,
the power to comprehend
the ugliness around you,
your belief, your
hope of peace.

And any day now, the rest:
what's left of your family, your friends,
your memory, your mind.

The woman you love.
You waited your whole life for her,
and now this.

THE LIGHT IN HERE
for Linda

If you resemble a mirror
you will be what you see,
the fundamental fragments.

Everything you remember
will be all you have lost,
and the light therein.

This thought revolves like the
last planet around the distant
light of our only sun:

a falcon hunting,
circling in the frozen air,
wings riding rings.

What is light to moth that jittery
moth must have its *jamais vu,*
the familiar unfamiliar?

From the 95th floor
I see the sparks of the city
laid out on the land.

There is fire in that wood.
There is light in this lamp.

BEACH

Gulls in the air,
looking for lift.

The fatal twilight,
a few late swimmers.

A baby cries out
for its mother's tit.

O body of water,
O body of bone!

A lone black stone
sits hunched in the sand

like a ruin around which
gather the dead.

'I have no ribbon to pretty this poem'

i have no ribbon to pretty this poem
when i leave it for you

so you'll find it
pinned to the table with a coffee cup

or under the magnet
on the refrigerator door

it's a little soft in the middle
a diminuendo before the grand finale

and it doesn't riff on anything big
like love or desire

in fact it's pretty small
as small as a blossom of baby's breath

i think you'll like it and smile
as you hold it in your hand and

god i love your loveliness
the way you have your way with the world

ABRAHAM REDUX

Late it was that the angel came
to relieve me of the mystery: the sweep
of the knife, the flood, the blooded blade—

the sacrifice that would have sufficed.
Earlier, as the sunlight broke across the hills,
I arranged my wood and Isaac I bound.

These were the steps. I took up the knife.
I could not look him in the eyes; instead,
my eyes like leopards studied Moriah

for any movement among the stone,
but I stood alone to bear in silence
the secret of the filicide, the fear

of what my hand was willing to do
on the altar. My wife knew nothing of
the plan, and when I returned I would need

to reconcile the grave contradiction
of belief and trust with the murder of her son.
I knew of no adequate defense.

Here I am an old man in a world dangling
by the slenderest silk, and I obeyed.
And in my freedom I obeyed, freedom to

condemn my son to the knife and the fire,
freedom even to refuse, if so I chose,
but what if I had refused, what then?

There's really no telling, but hell to pay.
And the world might not have turned on its needle
 and gone on spinning in just this way.

And the world would have forgotten me.
Yet had He seen fit to let me kill him
the world might have collapsed in singular

confusion, for none would have forgiven
the Name forbidden to the tongue of man.
Better the generations forgive me my faith.

Belong to me again, my son, whom I
would have killed. Behold the old silences, the
 dying fire, the whispers of the heart.

INSTRUCTIONS FOR SEEING THINGS

Consider the mountain that is not there.

Apprehend the flowers it left behind.

Say what you know, now that you know.

HANUKKAH HAIKU

In the hushed darkness
hovers the holy shamash.
Light touches white wick.

SUMMER SOLSTICE

This star we love, this only sun,
is of no constellation, and thus
it shines beyond imagining.

In the grass where we lay
in the warm sun, you said something.

Somewhere there is a light, I said,
in which all of your words survive, like stones.
Children will skip them on the glittering lake.

The Statue of Rene-Robert Cavalier,
Sieur de La Salle, Frenchman

Bronze La Salle
stands in the wilderness
above the street that bears his name.

His right boot rests
on the image of a tree-stump
across from the condominiums.

The handle of a flintlock
protrudes from his waistband,
and snowy his shoulders, and snowy the land.

His gaze is blind,
his eyelids heavy, and thus he sleeps,
and thus he wakes, his hollow mind receiving and

conceiving the winter's surfaces,
of which he himself is wholly a part,
himself foremost among those amplitudes.

THE GOD IN THE TREE

Up in the anvil of Illinois,
on a clear day in January,

the eye of a falcon
on the frozen branch

of an ash tree
in the shocking cold

tracks in its orbit
anything that moves.

Soon the falcon skreeks
and flies away,

vanishing in the
height of the sky,

leaving no trace,
no cause for inference.

The tree stands empty,
fixed in the wind.

We, the smallest of creatures,
sing often for less.

BOWL OF FRUIT

The bowl of fruit
is a revelation
to see it just so

the silver boat itself
no ... the fruit itself
the radiant apples

the just-so pears
floating in the moonlight
leaking into the dining room

or the glitter of light
wherever you are
dancing across the sea.

The Things You Find

Quarters between cushions,
cat's eye marbles under your bed,
your glasses in the bathroom,
a hungry kitten at your back door,
the clay bowl you made for your mother in 3rd grade,
a picture of your late brother David
riding his horse, Idle Mind,
leaning over the mane,
his spattered boots
hugging the chestnut's ribs.

Sometimes you get lucky
and find your way on a map,
a half-sister in Los Angeles
who bears a resemblance to you,
your way home,
and sometimes you find time for your daughter.

And you go on finding things
despite your weaknesses:
things in your heart
you never knew were there,
the courage to live
in opposition to the lie,
the value of that vacant x.

And what you've been looking for
for the longest time:
the right words,
the single path,
yourself.

The woman you thought you'd lost forever.
She forgives you like a river
that runs to the sea.

January

The heart of the night
is as white and as quiet
as a hunting owl.

It's so quiet even the wind
has nothing to say,
and the snow falls down.

After the transient rush
of a car down the street,
the owl sits in the silent world.

(Untitled)

The conversation turned to the past,
whether, having no moment, it even exists.
Yet the leaves fall, you said, we can see
them descending, dropping from the trees,
and they are become past, and as such
they gather. What lies ahead, then,
is the past, that which will have passed,
like the two blackbirds who were
here on the lawn not a moment ago.
I remembered the blackbirds there
in the grass, hunting, but mostly
I knew that the blackbirds had flown
toward a moment that can only recede,
toward that empty, uniquely vanishing point.
The past is the only thing that lasts.

THE FIFTH DECLENSION

Time to commit to memory
the final paradigm

I played football in the snow
and when I fell
I fell soft and white and low

nearly all of these nouns are feminine
genitive and dative are equivalent
accusative and ablative stand alone

standing alone waiting
for the kick
I commit to memory the path I'll take
through the falling snow

note that the plural forms
are uncommon
and do not resemble

a girl I love
watching me wind my white way
to score

all recite
let the mind conform

even then
I did it for love of her who saw
who stood with the snowflakes
dusting her hair

CHARLOTTESVILLE

Take me down to Charlottesville
as if to a river of baptismal fire
so that I may speak of the newly dead

and linger to grieve among the dogwood trees
for what has been born, born unto us.
What kind of alchemy turns gold into rust?

GO THERE AND BE

Go there and be, go anywhere.
If the sun shines, be warm.
If the clouds rain, be wet.
Go and breathe and
be what you be.

But hold your breath
if cardinals come
to redden the trees.
You'll be like a god
withholding his breeze.

CHIN MUSIC

The tv hanging above us on the wall
behind the bar bears a baseball game.
We're in from the heat, cold beer and a game
is all we require to cool our bodies
and seduce our souls. Every now and then,
the silent men advance a base or two,
but most of the time it's three up three down,
 a pitcher's duel developing, a beautiful
thing to watch, but the very next pitch
escapes the pitcher's grip, he releases it
too early, and it comes out wild and hard
and high and tight and cracks the batter just
above his left ear, the ball ricocheting
like a bullet toward the third base dugout.
The batter lies stunned on the ground near home plate,
with the team doctor hovering above him.
I was there when Conigliaro got hit, a guy
at the bar says. That was fucken horrible.
You have to respect that, and we do,
the same way you'd respect a Marine who bellied
 up a veteran of the the Battle of Khe Sanh.
Every pitch is thrown in anger, if you're serious
 about what you want to do.
The batter finally gets up, and they
walk him back to the dugout, where he
disappears down the ramp to the clubhouse.
The garne goes on, and it's still early
when we leave the bar, early enough to hear
the bells of St. Peter's signifying something,
ringing over the neighborhood, ringing,
the bells above us by bell-ringers rung.

POEM FOR MERLE

It was lovely seeing
you yesterday
throwing cardboard

boxes out by the
dented silver garbage
cans in the shadow

of the building on the
edge of the empty
parking lot.

Archaeology

There is always time and time
for the worlds of the world
to disappear, settling in dust,

or sliding back into the sea
on the backs of dolphins, or sacked outright.

Plato believed the dialectic sufficed
to discover the truth of lost Atlantis,
plunged in the terrible blindness

of the Atlantic, beyond the
pillars of Heracles, its warrior
kings of great and marvelous power

drowned upon their thrones.
The sea will keep the secrets of kings
safe from the philosopher's alchemy,

only some blind sailor drunk at his oar
tells how in the end those wine-dark waters
erupted and climbed and clashed with the stars.

ATLANTIS

There is always time and time
for the worlds of the world
to disappear, settling in dust,

or sliding back into the sea
on the backs of dolphins,
or sacked outright.

Plato believed the dialectic sufficed
to discover the truth of lost Atlantis,
plunged in the terrible blindness

of the sea, beyond the
pillars of Heracles, its warrior
kings of great and marvelous power

drowned on their thrones.
An image from *Mutus Liber* comes to mind:
a man fast asleep upon a rock,

limpid water pouring forth,
with two angels on the rungs of a ladder
blowing great horns in his ear to wake him,

and yet he sleeps as the world sleeps,
which must wake to rise and rise to find
the spiritual equilibrium.

The heavenly ladder doesn't reach to the sea,
which will keep the secrets of kings
safe from the philosopher's alchemy,

leaving only some blind sailor drunk at his oar
to tell how in the end those wine-dark waters
erupted and climbed and clashed with the stars.

SOCIAL MOBILITY

One can reinvent one's self,
turn from a tadpole, say, into a tarantula,
or something a bit more *de rigueur*.

It's the plan, in fact, for every American.
It's in the guidebook. *One must change:*
The kid carbuncular into the lady-slaying

poet, subject and object of his own mad art;
the flower on the dancehall wall into the
cosmologist sought after by smart men and dumb;

and on *ad infinitum*. But what of those who must stay put,
who lie deflected from life's grand occasion,
hopeless caterpillars grasping at metamorphosis?

I wish I could play soprano sax like Trane.
Man that kid can blow.

THE SWANS

I'm graveside again,
on a day glazed with not-quite rain,
to return her body to the Earth.

The pond is still here, and the pair
of swans who glide ghost-white
upon it, drifting through the mist.

I, like the oracle, have my faith
in birds, and read simulacra
commensurate with great puzzles.

Goodbye, sweet friend.
Forgive me this: that on your day
my grief shifted from you

to behold among so many dead
two swans who touched
in the center of a pond,

and there, meaning something just beyond
the swanlike, separated themselves
in space and time, the silence absolute.

LOVELIEST OF TREES

It's fine to consider
the cherry tree

when the SAC bomber drops
its big black pill

or even to see
that the thing we sent

bursts into bloom
like the loveliest of trees—

the cherry now
is hung with snow—

but that isn't knowing
what Nagasaki knew

when everything everything
everything blew

THE TREES OF EDEN

The sky holds the puny stars transfixed
like specimens pinned to a wall

but down here we are always moving
toward things and away from things

as if we ourselves had been
big-banged like buckshot

from that impossibly small
point of singularity

like when you said the trees of Eden
must have been very beautiful

and I moved toward you seduced
and began to move away from you

as soon as I touched
your beautiful face

THE DOLPHINS

I come to the edge of the western sea
to turn my back on the continent.
I've forgotten everything that lies behind me.
I cannot name those things anymore.

I see only the sea,
and the star at the end of the world
dropping behind the horizon.
The deep lungs of the sea swell and heave.

There is the dream that lies buried in sleep,
and there is the dream that finally wakes you
like a dolphin piercing the wine-dark sea....
The black sea dances with the last dazzling light.

The evening advances over the world.
The dream remains in the sea.
The dark dolphins plunge, and the dark dolphins breach.
Wake to the seagulls that circle and shriek.

WINTER ECLOGUE

A glance stolen like any other glance
was enough to lose Eurydice
after the ascent of Orpheus—

yet images accrue, the subject divides:
into all of winter's equations go
the dark unknowns of a possible whole.

Horses have walked across this white field
back to the barn, by their tracks. Here, all is
surface, hint and clue, guessed at, hidden and

hypothesized, but as I stand here with Orpheus,
one certainty: a cardinal fidgeting on an icy branch
is a drop of warm blood for that cold old man.

Even so, we move mostly among bloodless shades,
are drawn on and on by untraceable thirsts,
are haunted by the deaths our desires have wrought

until spring frees the flower from the marble of
 March. This I hold true, and thus I believe.
Go find Eurydice, of spring she will speak.

Home

No one noticed young Icarus falling
from the sun to the sea, and so no one
notices me wandering the streets and alleys
of my old neighborhood north of Chicago.
After years apart, I see it dimly,
but moments emerge: my first fight, here;
my first kiss of a pretty girl, here;
the first touch of whiskey to my tongue, there.

Many things are missing, of course, but
a revenant feeling remains. The bowling alley is gone,
the theater is gone, the amusement park gone,
and so on, ghosted. But I'm not here
to grieve the irretrievable past. Let that
which endures endure without too much fuss—
all else necessarily falls away. I've come
ambitiously for what I am. And so I walk.

I pick my way across the parking lot
of a supermarket, reading license plates,
then cross the field of the junior high
and follow a road of great promise:
the western light sliding down the slope
below the limbs and leaves of Grove Street
brings me down to my blonde brick home.
I did most of my living here, rashly and young.

I want to knock on the door of the old house
and ask the owner's indulgence. I have to know,
does my mother's magnolia tree still stand in the yard

after all this time, and has it blossomed yet this year?
The question begs the question; the tide withdraws,
 and lying there like a tarot card, the drowned youth.
And so it ends: it is something unfamiliar,
something else that thrives here now.

I don't, in fact, knock. I take a picture, two,
and give it one last look. The red paint
of the garage, the picture window overlooking
the wintergreens, the address sign I made in shop class,
the house of the widow Brooks next door.
It's all there, but not. I walk on a block or so
and come to the schoolyard where I might have played
softball in the spring, and football in the snow.

The yellow suburban light is fading now,
and soon the fall and the gathering of leaves.
I have fallen far on a sunny day,
unwilling to discover anything more.
I have moved uncertainly among my own,
and have stepped like a stranger on well-worn paths,
and have stood quietly among monuments of
 magnificent shadows, fountains of untraceable thirsts.

My Friend Lisa Speaks Briefly of Light

The morning
we descended,

the south side
lay like a grave

buried in clouds
except for three

thin ribbons of light.
That afternoon,

the sun in the yard
pinned silk strips

to the willow tree.
Later, walking along

the edge of the lake,
she says moonlight,

like the light of the eyes,
is as tragic as glass:

even a little water
will shatter it.

Deer

Decades ago, the Nature Center was
a sanitarium for those tubercular,
an art deco palace for the dying and dead.
I expected to find ghosts here,

but now it is mostly attended by deer
who move casually over the paths
beneath the tall angular windows.
The deer are gentle, but won't, I think,

approach the human hand,
preferring to linger under the trees,
touching their lips to the clover, or
straining for the lowest leaves.

One may reach conclusions, or not:
it is the deer emerging from the margin
of woods who bear the significance now,
nonhuman meaning in this once human place,

and I, an intruder from a vacated past,
come to rest at a stop sign, and there I wait,
extending to a doe through the car window
my empty white fingers, my ghostly white hand.

Los Angeles Divertimento

At three o'clock in the morning
the mockingbirds in the trees outside

were singing their little hearts out,
singing every song they knew.

I couldn't sleep, so I went for a walk
around the apartment. It was lovely

music the mockingbirds made,
and quite a repertoire, all the songs

of all the birds they had ever heard.
They were like prodigies at the piano.

I sat at my desk and thought
of Billie Holiday, the way

she made love to the vowels,
and I put on I'll Be Seeing You

and let Lady sing back to the mockingbirds.
Don't worry, I'll come back to bed, to you,

and touch your shoulder and kiss your ear,
and we'll wake late with our feet touching,

but now there are beauties commensurate
with the world of dream and sleep,

and it's me and the cat,
who was also something of a savant

(his gift was listening with an intensity
that surpasses understanding),

and here he is coiled on the window sill,
listening to the music outside in the trees

and Billie Holiday remastered.
It was just what both of us needed to hear,

something come from the nothing of night,
that moment awake, those notes in that life.

Daydream

I have no business here today
among the alder trees
leaning over the river.

Everybody knows it,
even the blackbirds.

I have things to do,
but I'm taking the time
to look at the river.

A thousand years from now
time will have bent it, but

now it's straight as a ruler,
sliding imperceptibly south to the vanishing point.

Two ducks
hitch a ride downstream,

but by the time I reach the Devon Avenue bridge
they are already invisible,
and the alder trees have disappeared,

and the great river itself
below my feet
has vanished, too.

What I Remember

when the towers in me came plunging down
and all those lives in you were lost

all life rubbed out in the fire and dust
of what was once us

you cried in front of the television
the same way my mother cried for kennedy

and I touched your arm
the same way I touched hers in '63

and later we wandered to holy name
and saw gypsies on the steps

playing barber's adagio for strings
a good place for grief the cathedral stood

enhanced by that cello and those violins
so sacred so necessary so achingly true

we were the only people left in the world
and would have cried out but for that music

Of Poetry

Let's be clear about this: Nature is dead,
its land, its seas, its unceasing sky,
like a walker in space who,
his umbilical cut, spins off in the vacuum
to revolve with debris.

Yet this river that draws a line through the city
has its history, as all lines do,
serves at least to enchant the memory,
and memory enchanted is a holy thing.
Let us still speak of the river, then,

not for the meaning it will no longer bear,
but with the feeling we reserve for serious things,
as we speak of a favorite aunt long since silenced,
or a dog we loved as children,
who still leaps through our dreams.

Babylon

Descending south through the plain of Shinar,
we come to the wreck of Babylon,
a few baked-mud ruins and revenant

echoes clinking the copper
of the captivity, all else scraped smooth
by a thousand winds. Why does the mind

spend its dream here, among hours made
holy by those same thousand winds?
What is the boar, the bull, or the owl

compared to us in our nightly stupor?
A dream, then, a human dreaming,
the eye lost in the darkness of sleep,

of a spontaneity of vivid gardens
hung for the pleasure of Hammurabi,
for his pleasure and the pleasure of all,

before dawn breaks between the rivers, and
we wake to the sacrifices, the old destructions,
the crumbling tower, the scattering of tongues.

CHICAGO PASTORAL

even here the falcon hunts
the high air under her wings
she floats and circles above the bungalows
the citiest of cities wakes on the wing

we look out from the kitchen on the yard
a card table a clothes line strung
over the lawn a few flowers
trembling in a bit of wind

everything depends on that image
or image of images ut pictura poesis
under a heap of old apartment buildings
let us again in the garden prove

yet things have rivered since we were young
 persisting in their identity
from the time of the sauk
down to our own desecrations

the river is as old as it ever was
and flowers come and flowers go
and the grass and lake and things go on
and we go on gazing out from the kitchen

and the falcon tips and turns and circles
above all the ugly bungalows

Because We Are Rivers

Because we are rivers, we see
what rivers see—
the branches of the alder trees
along the banks bristling
with red-winged blackbirds,
the sunlight breaking across the water,
the white boats
tugging at old pine docks.

Because we are rivers
we catch the sky, the clouds
drifting with us downstream
over the city heaped upon the land,
carrying the clouds
to the end of the line
where the heart slowly empties
into the sea.

Because we are rivers
nothing repeats,
things happen once,
the falcon is beheld;
thus the mysteries multiply
beyond the reach of reason,
each by each upon the ruin
wrought in iron and cement.

JERUSALEM

I went to Athens,
I went to Istanbul,
I went to Paris,
I went to Dublin,
I went to London,
I went to Tel Aviv.

She came to me in the old hotel
and we made love three floors above
the holiest ground,
a place of weeping
where we suffered
and where we wept.

Later, on the Via Dolorosa,
a decrepit old man said:
The dust that chokes you
in the pit of Hell
is the same dust that floats
in the eye of Heaven.

Outside the city,
the camels wait ...

One man with the truth
can ruin your life.

A Winter Scene

In the twilight over a crust of old
apartment buildings in West Rogers Park
the half-moon has risen, that hooded monk.

To discern the design of this the coldest
day of the year it helps to be fond of
black and white photography: all is laid bare

in the pale grey light, or half-buried there
like the Fords and Buicks and Oldsmobiles
and ash trees frozen in the falling snow;

or the river moving under the ice,
water to water in widening magnitudes,
down through the map where the rivers meet;

or the lone magnolia in the back yard,
impregnable, as hard as she will ever be,
like a wreck at the bottom of the sea.

Two women at the bus stop huddle and steam
like mares unbarned, chestnut and roan.
Two horses there change everything.

Spiritus Mundi

live like a ghost
in the home you inhabit

leave windows open
leave doors ajar

be the breeze
that lifts the curtain

rattle your keychain
at the ear of the dog

the tinkling in the other room
and the nighttime creak

of settling wood
is all your doing

light will pass through you
like onionskin

as you cast no shadow
across the kitchen floor

others will wonder
and investigate the mysteries

but don't explain
anything

you have become
wonder itself

you of all people
are not afraid

to wander like a rabbi
in his dark synagogue

The Walker

the tightrope walker makes his way
over the river
and the crowd
and the cameras below
like a bead on a string
one tender step

after another alone along the rigid rope
rooftop to rooftop
each footfall daring
catastrophe six
hundred feet above us

and halfway through the crowd hushes we hold
our breath
and behold
the master human
striding through the night
and every one of us

unwilling to defend the proposition that there are no mistakes
in the miraculous
anticipates a tragic finale

but he cast no shadow in that whirlwind nine minutes across
    and he never looked up
brooding like a god
on the face of the deep

My Friend Who Through The Gate Has Passed

My friend
   who through
      the gate has passed
like a mailman,
   says the soul
      is very small
and Heaven no more
   than a bungalow.
My friend who
   through the
      gate has passed
like white thread
   through the needle's eye
      says all of our lofty
imaginings are
   lovely and true.
My friend who through
   the gate
      has passed
like a drop of rain
   through
      a blinding fog
said upon his visit
   my blood beats
      because everything
is alive
   that close to the stars.

That Which Would Persist

My body was different
when I was small,

a playhouse for that
which would persist

as spirit or heart
and the music they hear,

and nothing was lost in me, e
verything found

according to those harmonies.
And words never uttered filled that hall:

lyrics and limericks and vaudevillian jingles,
and soliloquies followed by the drop of a pin.

And there was a dancing, too,
that body dancing in a desert on fire,

my Apache raindancer with his
turquoise and feathers,

an ancient art
that opens the clouds.

When it rains, remember
I've been dancing for you.

Thirteen Lines About The Fire In Wood

Something melts in the heart of winter.

A train streams from the mountainside tunnel.

The falcon waits in the walnut tree.

Beneath the ice you can hear the river.

Flames flare from a garbage can for two cold men.

The clouds are purple with the rain they hold.

Everywhere are flowers freed from the seed.

By lamplight we see the days dim and diminish.

 There is a woman in the body.

When she unpins her hair, the leaves fall.

There is a woman in the rose in the pale blue vase.

You take your hand from your pocket.

You touch the rose.

NIGHT
- after Rolf Jacobsen

In day we find night.
It's night in the cabinet,
under the couch it is night.
We don't need to look very far.
It's all around us.

Later,
when night comes into its own,
it will fall over your face,
a concealment,
like the last piece of a mystery
we don't really want solved.
That's when we flip switches,
or burn candles,
to drive it away.

And later still,
as you lie in bed
and close your dark eyes,
before your dreams
light you up inside,
the hammering of the heart
will have its say.
Always we begin
and end with the heart.

INCIDENT AT NAZARETH

Thomas Jeferson and his woman
rumbled up on his Harley.
The woman was blunt and hairy.

It was a good day for a ride, Thomas said,
swinging his leg over the saddle.
Not a fucken cloud in the sky.

The saloonkeeper, the dry-goods man,
and the mayor didn't want any trouble.

So they rode on. They rode all night
until they came to Nazareth.

VALENTINE

If I were to make a valentine for you
I'd begin and end with the things in the heart,

and between here and there
a dew-drenched rose,

and between this and that
the cool spray of the white waterfall,

but I'd also include
pictures of other things that you love,

like sea-bass and baseball,
or words to that effect.

See how, in its casual conjuring,
the imagination finally fails?

This happens every time
I fall in love with you.

WHAT IS IT THAT TAKES YOUR BREATH AWAY?

Is it the sublimity of the rumbling sea,
or the canyon-cutting river,
or the smaller beauty of the blood-red rose?

I cannot comprehend the sea,
and I do not understand the river,
so I'll go with the red flower, for love,

because I believe in completely
the beads of rainwater
on the skin of the rose

at the farthest transport of the imagination,
beyond the white visions
and breezy golden fields,

beyond, finally, the mind
and its inklings, with no need
of the mind's profundum.

Faith in a single, simple rose,
and faith in its image
long after it withers.

A WORD

I wrote a word and lost it
in a parking lot.

Maybe some shopper would find it
and consider the mystery,

but that's not what happened.
In the spring I saw it

on the branch of a tree
leaning out over the river.

I don't really care how it got there
because it was like a red-winged

blackbird now, fidgeting among
the common sparrows

on the sagging branch,
before it flew off and just after.

ELECTION

Suspended, our nominees point to make points
from the tv hanging on the wall.

Oh we need to know a thing or two,
the impassive among us most of all.

(To grasp the time and the time's passion
is all the rage, in rags or high fashion).

We have sacrificed everything for this—
our primitive rituals, our magic tricks,

and if we want more,
battlefields are rich in our own blood and gore.

(The one advantage to growing older
is that eventually one grows colder).

A MIRAGE

In the distance where the road rises
an image is given

shivering in the haze,
in the sun-shocked heat.

When I get there it's nothing,
a mirage that has vanished.

I drive right through it,
like a dolphin through the sea.

Myth, speak to me no longer
to tantalize me with your tales-

I think I'm here to tell what I see
and no more.

On Schnittke's 'Collected Songs Where Every Verse is Filled with Grief'

If I were equal to the things I know,
if all distances collapsed,

I'd be my body, that broken stone,
smooth and marble and whole.

The planet also is fractured and small,
sailing on with her many sorrows,

unlike the solid god as she rolls
and rolls through the emptiness,

the horrible emptiness
His vast vectors pierce.

The space between notes,
then, the space that shapes music,

is the space between us,
the space that shapes us.

It's like dying alone.
There lies the grief

Now That I Am Old

Now that I am old
shall I invoke old spells

or let come the syllables of the heart
to intrude upon an evening?

I think of the ghost of my desire
who haunts this dominion,

and the anguish of language left behind,
held back like breath,

and in the darkness surrounding the rose
I consider what I have felt for you,

a black and white dream where things appear
to last forever, a tired tableau,

a bowl of silver moonlit fruit, a case of old books,
until I come to the rose in the vase,

the sacred rose and its red magnitudes,
red-rich and reaching across the years.

IF DEATH COMES BLACK

If death comes black
like dreamless sleep,
I guess I'll have to go;

if death comes green
like newly mown grass,
I guess there's room to grow;

if death comes white
like a radiant bride
cutting her wedding cake,

the cherry trees
in fanatical bloom
will light my way like snow.

Seder

In Los Angeles I heard mockingbirds
whistling in the trees, as it is said,
articulating night with songs overheard
of songbirds near the sea by the hills,
near the coming and going of the sea.

And so it was with my ancestors
walking through the sea, as it is said,
light from the troubled sky once more
to reveal the seabirds crying out,
to show the waves of seawater roll.

And so to that which would have sufficed:
the mockingbirds once again at my ear
singing of the sorrows in the heart
and of the heart's vast departures, as it is said.
 Pierce me like dolphins pierce the wine-dark sea.

Setting Out

I'm driving in the drizzle.
In the grass to the side of the highway,
a red-tailed hawk battles a rodent.
My old high school stretches out like a freight train.
I know less
than a man asleep in the straw
of an empty boxcar,
who dreams of California,
perhaps, and
beyond.

Afternoon Prayer

Behold, there are those who sleep in the dust,
whose particles of faith didn't quite coalesce
around the larger theme of certainty,
who doubted small and doubted large but with love
 for the idea of the nameless one,
of the first and last possibility,
the center of heart and awakening,
beyond the old reckoning, beyond the
final horizon where the sea meets the sky,
and, constantly rendering a something
from nothing, are the secret envy of
the steadfast and true, for they apprehend
and see what they doubted, so may we trust.
Blesséd are those who sleep in the dust.

The Body In Rebellion

My body, Mann,
has served me well
but now deserts me
piece by piece
less and less
each morning
to fuck around
with scrambled eggs
and cigarettes and
confounded by mysteries
like limbs that itch
which no longer exist
I look to the rivers
and when they dry up
the rivers that run into
and from the heart
which withers
like a cut rose
I will miss
everything
most of all

To His Coy Mistress

Hold my hand, and close your eyes,
and come with me to the river.
Let others look to the holiest seer.
We'll find passage in the stars
with the end of the world so near.

The Eye of the Beholder

I couldn't find anything on this street
that would flee like beauty—
not the drab four-flats,
not the rigid rows of undistinguished cars,
not the empty winter sky.

Then a coal-black squirrel
came hopping over the snow.
He was magnificent, like a black Ferrari.
When our eyes met, he put the pedal to the metal
and fled to the dark side of the moon.

August Comes to an End

It's been raining for days.
There's a woman in my room.
She has a Caesarean scar.

She lights her cigarette from my cigarette.
We can hear the rain pecking at the window.
The silence between us isn't what you think.

We've already talked.
Now we're at rest, listening to the sound
the rain makes on our skin.

Exodus

Though east kill west and
light put out light shall rise again from the sea
to reveal the seabirds crying out
to see the waves of seawater roll.

Though dark we are in the blinding sun
sound shall see us through the night
to hear the song of the mockingbirds
whistling in the trees.

Though for us to feel in such fatal light
is more than they can bear
outwardly we shape this form of flesh
from the sorrow in the heart.

Though the salt of France's dead is fresh
 on our speechless tongues
a voice shall rise from the lungs of the sea
where the waves of water part.

'Again The Fall'

Again the fall
and its intimations of death

the leaves for instance drop
and we walk among them

rehearsing our beliefs
dust to dust etc.

the breath we see steaming away
the body we conceal

the mind that connects the dots
the soul that waits

and soon that final cruelty
and I a ridiculous fool

who risked too little too late
a stick figure

planted before the cold
waiting for it to come and go

waiting to cross
waiting for the light to change

A Ship Off Oranjestad

I sit and mildly dream,
in a red leather chair,
of a ship I saw off Oranjestad,

which is with me now,
as present as this parakeet,
golden in his dream of parakeets

underneath his night shade.
The two of us board the ship,
bound for Patagonia.

There are no other passengers,
only a skeleton crew
and a captain hidden in his quarters.

Neither of us know anything
about our journey,
or our destination,

or why we're going there.
At sea in the morning,
two days out,

I free the parakeet
to soar in high winds
over the surging Atlantic.

After an hour or so,
he comes home to the great ship,
like a yellow leaf falling to Earth.

Autumn Aubade

Like a technicolor lighthouse, mademoiselle,
the eye sheds light on the things it observes,
and so it sheds its long color on you:

that's you under the beige muslin of fog
 covering this rustling red river of you;
that's you sliding past a tarnish of trees

empty of this year's iteration of green;
and when you dawn again, blinking and white,
the sum of all colors in Illinois,

I will tell you how through the window
the sinking moon, struck blue by the beam,
fell and fell and fell blue over you.

Something

If I must have a god,

let it be You
and your atmospheric blue

Your
streak of cloud in the eastern sky

Your
fire of sun and ashes of moon

You
and your wiggle room

Your
geometry Your point and line

Your
vast vectors of the grand design

Your
equations and evasions

and You
empty as a crumpled coat left on a bench

silent in space

less than a ghost who rattles his chain

but Something

AIDS WARD, CEDARS SINAI HOSPITAL, LOS ANGELES, 13 MAY 1994

This is where David has come to die
and this is where we have gathered.
He lies there in a spasmodic coma
which means his limbs move and rise,
his arms outstretched as though to greet you.
He has lingered and lingered here by the sea,
but he'll be gone with the morning light.
It's dark in the room and we're taking turns
with him, so he's not alone, so we can say
anything we need to say. It's my turn and I tell him
 to go see daddy and go see nanny, gone so many years.
Maybe they're there waiting for David.
Who can say what lies hidden in heaven,
but in the heat of dying nobody here cares.
David's forehead is on fire from the meningitis.
And his friend Hank, bitterly, who walks
with a cane because he has a hole in his heart:
Thank you God for this wonderful gift, called HIV.
I tell my mother I'll put a pillow over his face
and suffocate all the misery in a single embrace,
but she says no, no, he's my baby.
I never told my sister about that.
He's my little brother and we played together.
 Someone sent flowers to the room yesterday.
One of his friends lights a candle.
There is no music to listen to, no
Barber's Adagio, no Gorecki's Third Symphony

to tell us what we're feeling. How does one feel
about such a thing without appropriate music?
The nurse says this is how a body shuts itself down,
and the morphine dripping into his arm.
He'll be gone with the morning light.
We'll all be gone with the morning light.